The Whimsical Crime
of Rhythm and Rhyme

Gail P. Robertson

The Whimsical Crime of Rhythm and Rhyme

ISBN: 978-0-9921203-2-0

This book is dedicated to
the Cowichan Valley Arts Council,
the arts and culture 'go-to' place in this region
of Vancouver Island, British Columbia, Canada.

Cover art by Gail P. Robertson

TABLE OF CONTENTS

I started writing poems in my youth. I've hung onto them all these years, and finally, some have found their way (updated, of course) into this, my first book of poetry.

Each one tells a story, entertains or engages the intellect. To me, rhythm and rhyme are an integral part of the charm which this form of prose has to offer.

Please enjoy . . . .

PART I: Whimsy and Wacky

I find the best way to look at life is with a humorous twist. Drollery can certainly put things in a different light, a healthier perspective. And sometimes, ordinary things are quite amusing, or at least of a whimsical nature, when observed from the outside looking in.

Here are a few examples which tickled my fancy, and may amuse you as well.

THE POET'S HAND

To write a poem is not as easy as it may sound –
Confound!
To make lines rhyme is not as simple as all that –
Drat!
Your leaky pen makes my fingers black and gooey –
Phooey!
This blank paper shows your failure to produce –
Duce!
This poised hand shakes; how long will this last? –
Blast!
And what if this brain concocts a hundred verses –
Curses!
And in each line tries a hundred words to cram –
Damn!
Well, brain, this hand is about to rebel:
I'm getting a cramp, and you can go to –
Hell!

CANINE'S AGENDA

Trip a person, chase a cat,
Chew a shoe, tear a hat,
Unpot a plant, unearth a bone,
Unmake a bed, unhook the phone.

Break a vase, wet the rug,
Steal a treat, sniff a bug,
Bark at neighbors, scare a child,
Dig up gardens, nap awhile.

Topple trashcans, soil the clothes,
Ruin some brand-new pantyhose,
Pull the stuffing from the couch,
Get a scolding from a grouch.

Mooch from people, drool and sneeze,
Give a happy home to fleas,
Spill his water, slop his food –
And today, he's being *good!*

CAT HOLIDAY

The cat could think of many ways
That she'd prefer to spend her days –
To eat or nap, undo a hem . . .
A kennel wasn't one of them.

She'd been in there the year before
And knew it was again in store.
The bustle as the humans packed,
Of cat abandonment it smacked.

So when they opened up the door,
She left! They'd see her nevermore.
A new home now she had in mind,
With someone older, someone kind,

Who understood her growing need
For comfort food, soft post to knead,
And perches high enough that she
Could look aloof and almighty.

It mustn't be a canine realm,
No other cats be at the helm,
And certainly no babes or kids
Who she would have to live amidst.

Her freedom was most sacrosanct,
And she must not be spanked
If they'd her playful side outgrown
Or she brought 'groceries' of her own.

She wandered for a mile or more,
Then crossed the yards, from door to door.
The smells there a dead givaway
Of what beyond the thresholds lay.

Before too long, naptime was nigh,
Someplace where she'd be warm and dry,
Dream of a soft and cushioned bed,
House where she'd be watered and fed.

She briefly thought of going home
For one more meal before she'd roam,
But how quick would she have to be,
Come morn, to remain free?

She sighed and quickly looked around,
For hidey-holes always abound.
Weed-overgrown, but padded swing,
Proved to be just the perfect thing.

She woke, for it was getting dark,
And nearby heard a canine bark.
She slipped down from her cushy perch,
And for some dinner went to search.

Unwary mouse in field well-grassed
Provided adequate repast.
An absent dog's big water bowl
Served both her thirst and cleansing goal.

Ancestral habits now kicked in
From ancient, prehistoric kin.
Perhaps she'd just live off the land,
Foreswear annoying ties to man.

A feral cat forever be,
Living as wits and stealth decree.
No one to tell her what to do.
She'd bid the 'easy life' adieu.

Late autumn nights were chilling down,
Soon snow would be upon the ground,
Her prey would become hard to find,
And secure shelter to unwind.

Lately, her thoughts kept sliding back
To what she'd left, and what she lacked.
Was one emprisonment a year,
Worth all this hassle, risk and fear?

Unerringly, her paws set forth,
A bit this way, and then true north.
A few days' trek it took to spot
The very house she'd valued not.

With journey's end within her sight,
She meowed, then yowled with all her might,
Until the door flew open wide,
And she just hurtled deep inside.

Then they were hugging her with cries
Of happiness, and weepy eyes.
Soon she was feasting on the best
Meaty cat treats she'd e'er possessed.

Now with a deep, contented sigh,
She chose her favorite place to lie.
Though great adventure t'was to roam,
Noplace out there could rival home.

I'M A QUITTER

I'm a quitter.
I'm anything but a go-gitter,
Just flittering hither and thither,
But batting a lifetime no-hitter,
'Cause I'm a quitter.
I start an invention, then stop it;
Take up the guitar, and then drop it.
My only achievement is quitting.
I quit in the midst of most any–
I'm a quitter.

I'm awake at the breaking of dawn,
Aching to rise and be gone
In search of my fortune and fame,
And to immortalize my own name.
To cut me a piece of the pie,
And sow me a patch of the sky,
To do things that have never been done.
Straw into gold to be spun.

Blessed with divine inspiration
(Bordering on desperation),
I charge in – full speed ahead!
I could slave until I drop dead.
But as I'm approaching the middle,
I begin to tinker and fiddle,
And the closer it gets to be finished,
The more my excitement's diminished.

By the time the end is in sight,
I'm ready to quit for the night,
Knowing well that by the next morning,
The whole thing will seem much too boring,
And a far more interesting project
Will seem a more lucrative prospect,
And the garage will claim yet more litter,
The mark of the compulsive quitter.

ROCKHOUNDS

What species of madfolk can sometimes be found
Tearing down structures for decorative stones?
Appropriately known to the world as 'rockhounds',
They're persistent as a dog who's after a bone.

No meadow is sacred, no stream is too deep.
They'll pluck stones from patios and rock gardens.
If your house seems to tilt a wee bit while you sleep,
There's a hole in your foundation (beg your pardon).

From the beaches and quarries to sheerest cliffsides,
Choice rocks are no good 'less they've got 'em.
And they've started some calamitous rockslides,
Just to get at that one at the bottom.

A pawn of compulsion, they continue their searches,
Their trophies displayed on the shelf
In their tilting homes. These precarious perches
Reveal their addiction. I'm a rockhound myself.

CHRISTMAS EVE

A certain Christmas evening,
Careening 'tween the stars,
An E.T., looped on moon-juice,
Missed the turnoff cue for Mars.
His sky-skidoo demolished
That point upon the Earth
Where Santa's sleigh awaited,
Though all escaped unhurt.

But lacking transportation,
And badly pressed for time,
Santa outlined his proposal
With gestures, grunts and mime.
The Martian wheezed his consent,
Bade Santa climb aboard,
Got his battered spaceship whirring,
And through the night they roared.

Deep-sounding like a dolphin,
And pickled to the gills,
The Martian tried to show off
And land on windowsills.
Told *rooftops* were his target,
He left a shattered trail
Of chimneytops and weathervanes
And tiles and tin and nails.

Before the night was over,
No stone was left unturned,
No house was left untarnished,
No barn was left unburned.
But justice finally triumphed,
And he lost his 'aero' bars.
Now he's flying from a cannon
In the Circus of the Stars.

VIOLENCE

We sit before our televisions quietly
Listening to the evils of our society.
But the violence that we hear of every day
Is reflected in the savage things we say.

People like it when you crack a smile.
Kick a habit, to a nun, must sound vile.
And no one likes to see you killing time.
Break a promise, and your word ain't worth a dime.

It hurts to see ideas bite the dust,
But trying to beat inflation is a must.
We strike a match or devour a tasty snack,
And come nightfall, peacefully hit the sack.

It's the same when you're hearing office talk.
Everybody has to punch the clock.
They push a pencil and the phone they tie up,
Waste paper and slit open envelopes.

They attack problems, and beating them's a treat.
Why, I've even seen policemen pound a beat!
If you're shocked by the lives the workers live,
Wait till you hear about executives!

Of a merger they plot to split the cost.
Price freezes, sales pitches, paper embossed.
They stretch a point and then they bend the rules.
Now, is that what they're taught in business school?

The things we do in leisure time for fun
Is bad enough, like murdering a song.
We drown a thirst and blithely shoot the breeze,
Chase a rainbow, crash a party, if you please!

You wonder how some people cannot feel.
Why, sadists even make their tires squeal.
Jokers crack up audiences, and I
Have heard a man make a violin cry.

And so, as I was churning out this thought
I deigned to give self-righteousness a shot.
Now I spout the very speech that I eschew!
Turns out I'm every bit as bad as you.

THE TIME-SNUBBERS

Here's to the folks who are never on time,
Eternally tardy, consistently blind
To that bastion of time, ye local Big Ben,
You hope they'll be there, but you never know when.

Rash adventurers defying the almighty clock,
No slave to time, they run blissfully amok,
Simply living life as their free spirits decree,
Quite content just to follow their olfactory.

For surprise birthday parties, they're invariably late,
If you wait dinner for them, they already ate.
Incorrigible lateness is an incentive to crime,
Driving friends to kill them ahead of their time.

It's totally pointless to meet the Greyhound or train,
As you'll have made the trip for nothing, again.
Timetables must be what they gave up for Lent,
For getting there on time would be sheer accident.

Chronic procrastinators, take heed and beware,
For the clock-watcher people abound everywhere.
Being late throws a wrench in our ordered chaos,
You're vastly outnumbered, so surrender and join us.

THE ULTIMATE WEAPON

In a peaceful-looking building
On a lazy country lane,
Agricultural scientists
Were at it once again.
Totally committed to
An insecticidal war,
They built the Ultimate Weapon
The world was waiting for.

Like Holy War crusaders,
With 'Right' they went out armed,
Intending to annihilate
The scourge of the farm:
The voracious caterpillar:
Insatiable appetite –
A walking, wiggling stomach,
Eating everything in sight.

They located a fine specimen
On which 'X' they could test
To see how very quickly
It would destroy this pest.
With infinite caution, they
Placed one drop near his head,
And the smell drew him toward it,
Though his eyes were turning red.

The caterpillar touched it, as
They watched with bated breath,
And went into what they took for
His final dance of death.
At last, he lay completely still,
With one brief, erratic sigh,
And the scientists noted he had taken
Ten scant seconds to die.

But soon after they departed
To fill in their report,
The caterpillar got up
To take another snort.
Never had he felt so high,
So drunk, so strong, so free,
Not since he'd got a whiff of
That outlawed DDT.

Fe, fi, fo, fum – we will kill those pests, by gum!
Fe, fum, fo, fi – on the ground and in the sky.
Fe, fum, fi, fo – your goodies make us stronger grow.
Fum, fo, fi, fe – next stop: immortality.

THE MASHER

Eeeek! You horrendous little blackguard!
You malicious little sneak!
To have given my innocuous
Little bottom such a tweak!

To demean my virtuosity
And treat me like a slut.
Pull a sneak attack behind my back
And pinch me in the butt.

For such sacrilegious treatment
Of sanctimonious me,
You deserve some fancy footwork
To your masculinity.

And though it much behooves me
To use words so crude and crass,
If you ever touch my form again
I'll kick your bloody ass.

THE CARNIVORERS

The idyllic year Three Thousand,
And the world's abolished war.
Disease is almost unknown.
Life is boring but secure.

Organized crime is passé,
Newscasts hold no horrors,
But a new Prohibition
Has outlawed Carnivorers.

The disgusting social illness
Of ingesting animal flesh.
Feasting on forbidden filet
Can intern you for a stretch.

But reckless venizen smugglers
Are stalking wild beefsteaks,
Dreaming of grilled buttocks
Instead of spinach pancakes.

Retched relics of yesteryear
Yearn with all their hearts
To dine just one more time
On choice mammalian parts.

And maybe, if they're lucky
They'll devise a time machine,
And join us happy savages
Gnawing Angus or Holstein.

CARPENTRY 101

There once was a house on the side of a hill
That was built by a man with a little less skill
Than was needed to make it a permanent dwelling,
And no one was buying the tale he was selling.

So he took up his hammer and took up his saw,
And walled up what seemed the most visible flaw.
Though the rickety door he was trying to hide
Was now firmly secure, there was no way inside.

So he sawed a new hole for a door to go through
Inadvertently cutting a hole in the flue.
And in fixing the chimney, the roof sagged a bit,
Thus compelling some timbers that held it to split.

With the floor joists vibrating, he walked down the hall
To inspect cracks that ran the whole length of the wall.
As the house started swaying, he yelled to his wife
To get the heck out, then he ran for his life.

He surveyed the rubble, unable to guess
How it all ended up such a horrible mess.
"The pictures looked easy," he muttered, upset.
"You can learn any trade on the Internet."

DEMOCRACY

I understand democracy –
All about 'life' and 'liberty' –
But when I pursue Happiness,
Happiness runs away from me.

And Happiness flees like the wind,
But I can run faster than she.
And when I find Happiness,
The police come and arrest me.

I love her, but she won't see me,
So I woo her like in Old Country.
I put a ladder to her window,
So her father will not know.

I wake her up romantically.
I kiss her hand so tenderly.
I whisper, "Now we elope, please?"
She look at me and scream, "Police!"

Now her father wants my life.
The police want my liberty.
Your Honor, I am in this mess
Through the pursuit of Happiness.

PART II: Under the Microscope

I'm taking a chance here, because our perspective on a subject says more about us and our frame of mind at the time than it does about the topic itself. But sometimes, when we emotionally put ourselves in a picture, it also increases our empathic understanding of what we're describing.

Let's see what you think . . .

SPRING

Buds and flowers and April showers,
And Springtime's coming to town.
Apple blossoms and skimpy costumes
Scenery abounds.
People grinning, the world is spinning
In time to a different tune.
Winter's done and everyone's a buffoon.

Birds are singing, the Spring is springing
And love's blooming everywhere.
Days are longer, our hearts beat stronger,
Devil-may-care.
Elevating, we're celebrating
'Cause Winter's again far astern.
Sweet and snappy, and many happy returns.

ANATOMY OF A DAY

Elements of Nature, in
The cauldron of our fates,
Have wed and incubated
This most luxurious day.
Percolating through the trees,
Sunwebs, arrow-straight,
Intersperse with shadows to
Form Nature's macrame.

Rubbernecking right along,
With Time my willing slave,
Selecting scenes to feed my
Treasure-trove of memories.
A summer breeze breaks over me
Like an ethereal wave,
These sunkissed hours just brimming
With life's little ecstacies.

The dead of night will also be
The demise of today,
Its elements returning to that
Melting, smelting pot.
Recombined, revitalized,
They sculp the coming day:
A stage on which life's games
Will be either played or fought.

NIGHT

The sky is losing its war with the night,
As the Dark One gorges on its life's-light.
Wings of darkness envelop its victim,
And only the morning can rescue him.

The world's timid people feel the onslaught of dread,
And cringe from the shadows that surround their bed.
They wonder what's causing that creaking downstairs,
And feel their flesh crawl and their rising neck hairs.

For strange things occur in the dead of the night,
When the world is deprived of its power of sight.
The primeval instincts of hunter and hunted,
Day's civilization becomes night's jungle instead.

Long before midnight, the town comes alive,
The environment in which the night people thrive.
Casinos and floor shows, at bars or a dance,
They search for excitement, adventure, romance.

With darkness their matrix, the background they choose
To offset and highlight kaleidoscope hues,
Night folks make strobe lights and neons their sun.
When our day is over, theirs has only begun.

The timid and night folk see the coming of dawn,
The first with relief, the second sad night is gone.
In a few fleeting hours, time will repeat the spell,
And one will find heaven in the other one's hell.

TIME

Time – at once our enemy and our friend,
Healing wounds, but guiding us to our end.
A packrat in a never-ending race,
Steals from us, but leaves something in its place.

Our lives lie beyond, on a slow-moving ramp.
Housed in the present, we cannot decamp.
The door to the past permits only the dead,
And a shroud of fog veils the future ahead.

An obstacle course with no pitfall or prize
Visible beforehand, or its value disguised,
We must pick our paths without even a glance
At the repercussions, in this game of chance.

Though the setbacks be many and the successes few,
We still rue the day when our life will be be through.
Life is a treasure to be borrowed, not kept,
And Time the most precious gift we accept.

HALLOWE'EN

The witches and the skeletons,
The vampires and the ghosts
Will be out in force tonight,
Literally coast to coast.

Attired in ghoulish costumes,
Their laughter fills the night,
The sights and sounds of Hallowe'en
That give children such delight.

The adults are invited to
Dress up, not just the youth.
Join happy intertwining
Of fairy tales and truth.

A little added atmosphere
From a kindly hostess witch.
Candy exchanges hands amid
Her cackle, weird, high-pitched.

Kaleidoscopic memories
So simply given birth
Will long outlast the treats devoured
With reminiscent mirth.

This candy is available
Each day of every week.
It's impromptu entertainment
And adventure children seek.

CHRISTMAS EYES

The season befalls young and old,
The year into history flies,
Warmth of heart, despite the cold
As we gaze through Christmas eyes.

For many, ancient tale retold,
Baby's birth and rulers wise.
Their re-enactment to unfold
And reinforce religious ties.

The merchants help the list we hold
Translate in costly buys.
Our pleasures bought, their treasures sold,
A packaged love in gift disguise.

We see dear friends and neighbours stroll
By, who we greet with happy cries.
Hugging, smiling, hearts behold
The festive spirit now reprised.

Presents in wrapping paper mold,
Hidden lest they spoil surprise,
Worth far more than precious gold
To kids awaiting Santa's prize.

The tree long dressed in colours bold,
Gift paper shreds in glad demise
To squeals of delight no one scolds,
The scene cherished through Christmas eyes.

GOLD FEVER

The autumn wind blustered sharp and cold,
Penetrating their clothing with ease,
As the partners panned the stream for gold,
Wooing Lady Luck on bended knees.

The months of toil had taken its toll,
Their vacant eyes held but despair.
Their rainbow's end held no pot of gold,
What they'd built their dreams on wasn't there.

With unseeing eyes they searched the silt,
Each dreaming of a wife or girlfriend,
Each realizing, with pangs of guilt,
His promise of gifts would be broken.

The icy stream chilled them to the bone,
As winter approached with measured stealth.
Penniless, they faced hardships yet unknown,
Garbed in poverty instead of wealth.

A single scream has slashed the gloom.
Gone the water, the wind and the pain.
GOLD! They are snatched from the mouth of Doom
To the land where sunshine reigns again.

CALENDRIALLY SPEAKING

What month always dawns cold as hell,
With ice felling the unwary?
Three months 'till Spring breaks Winter's spell.
That's right; it's January.

February's only fit for
Hibernation or winter sports,
Or lounging on some tropic shore.
Thank goodness February's short.

Born to a world of ice and snow,
March also hears early birds sing.
Though arriving painfully slow,
We see the first true signs of Spring.

April showers, nectar of Spring,
Washes away lingering snow,
Awakens an earthful of seedlings,
Which busily begin to grow.

It's partly mild and partly cold,
Like a seasonal tug-of-war.
Flowers and grass, precious as gold,
May is what we've been waiting for.

Strawberries and earthly delights,
Summer fun, June's gentle breezes.
Nature's heyday, the year's highlight.
Joie-de-vivre that never ceases.

July is like a happy child,
Discovering summer's treasures.
Rosy complexion, sunshine smile;
Being alive is a pleasure.

Hazy August, lazy August,
Summer curls up and takes a nap.
The reeds are red as copper rust,
And life tastes sweet as maple sap.

An Autumn crispness nips the air,
Pinching leaves to colored splendor.
Summer dies, with visual fanfare.
A month of change is September.

It's Hallowe'en and pumpkin pies.
It's tart and tangy as a spice:
October. Despite graying skies,
The aging year can still be nice.

The year is nearly done, so we
Reminisce, and we remember
Good times in recent history,
Including this month: November.

Hustle and bustle, Christmastime,
Parties and snow, and the year's end.
Like a familiar nursery rhyme,
New Year's . . . and here we go again!

POLITICKING

Hear my words and see my smile,
I have flair, panache and style.
I'll do much more than they can,
'Cause I've got a better plan.

Vote for me, and not the rest.
I'm the chosen, I am blessed.
Every promise will come true.
I'll do everything for you.

It cost more than we could guess.
Our predecessors left a mess.
It'll take a lot more time –
But our plan is working fine.

Election time has come again.
We're experienced now, my friend.
Splendid job we did for you.
We'll do better next time, too.

See the goodies that you'll get.
Vote for us with no regrets,
And ignore the pics and tapes.
They're falsified or sour grapes.

All those things I never said,
Were misquoted. They mislead
You to think we did you wrong.
See my dance, and hear my song.

INFINITY

I'm the path you'll walk tomorrow,
I'm the ghost of yesterday.
Though your instruments record me,
They can't stop me slipping 'way.
Through the centuries you've counted,
Noting down religiously
Every second, minute, hour;
You're preoccupied with me.

You can't see them, you can't feel them,
Equal portions left behind.
They are falling off too quickly
To perceive, the dots of time.
How you use them is your proxy,
To be spent but never kept.
They disintegrate on passing,
Lacking height and width and depth.

I am everywhere in sequence,
Blank slide frames, all lacking sides.
Not a judge and not a jury,
I observe but do not guide.
Every thing consists of substance,
Changing form infinitely.
Substance dies, but time lacks substance,
So I am Infinity.

THE SWEET AND SIMPLE THINGS

Then I knew where I was going,
Getting closer all the time.
My fondest dream could be bought with a dime.
And a million great adventures
Were as close as a daydream,
And I could catch a whale in our own stream.
Chocolate cake could cure most anything,
And a boy could become king.
How I miss the sweet and simple things.

All the fireflies were pixies,
Playing catch-me-if-you-can.
Summer nights I camped out on the land.
Fell asleep to songs of bullfrogs
And the wind among the pines.
Life would always be my valentine.
How I'd search for hidden treasure,
And today it seems a crime,
'Cause now I know I had it all the time.

THE RAINS

The kids will have to stay indoors,
Content themselves with games and trains.
The mother sighs, for she deplores
This gloomy week of constant rain.

The Maasai and wild animals
Rejoice as drought ends on the plains
And celebrate the coming squalls –
Salvation by life-giving rains.

The owners watch with growing fear
As rising waters put more strain
On levies built the previous year
To hold back flooding from the rain.

The desert creatures rush about
A landscape now rare color-stained,
For food and water sources scout,
Delivered by the recent rain.

The mudslide buried half the town;
Catastrophe had struck again,
The hill transformed to barren ground,
All caused by the relentless rain.

The seasons come and seasons go;
The weather patterns wax and wane.
Though we may call it friend or foe,
We're subject to the falling rain.

THINK IT OUT

Did you ever sit and talk
To a cloud or to a rock?
Did you ever reach that point of true despair,
When anything would do
As something to talk to?
A cry for help spoken to thin air.

And the rock, in solitude,
Seemed so strong and solid, too;
Strong enough to bear your problem's weight.
And that cloud, so soft and free
Might understand your misery;
The answer from its mists might emanate.

Sometimes the need to explain
Some deep emotional pain
Can lead you to do things that look quite daft.
For the clouds and rocks can't hear
Or help allay your fears
But when you speak, they, at least, won't laugh.

Caught in a web of dreams
And home-made half-baked schemes
In truth as stifling as a lie.
You tore your wings on clouds,
And now must join the crowd
Of people who have set their sights too high.

Think it out, or you're never gonna fly.

WAKEY WAKEY

Wakey, wakey; frosty morn.
Another chilly day is born.
Time to rise and go outdoors
To tend the cows and muck the floors.

Just do the chores one final time,
Then wash away the stable grime.
New owners will arrive at noon.
It will be their decision soon.

So bid the farm routine adieu.
You made a goal and saw it through.
It's time to start another life
In which I'm not a farmer's wife.

For you and I, the future calls,
So say goodbye to those old stalls.
We're headed for a warmer place
And lifestyle with a slower pace.

I know it's feeling bitter-sweet,
But I, for one, won't miss the sleet,
The early mornings or the snows,
Or droughts or floods or insect woes.

No matter how our life unfolds,
In comfort let us both grow old.
With travel, hobbies, newfound friends,
We won't miss barnyard denizens.

So feed the chickens, lock their gate.
A hearty breakfast will await.
The years of toiling came and went,
Time to embrace retirement.

CASINO

Casino games, perchance to win.
Some call it fun, some call it sin.
We roll the dice or spin the wheel,
Bet on slots or on the deal.

Scratch-off tickets, sporting bets,
Lotteries or bingo sets.
Each devised to grab our buck
As we are wooing Lady Luck.

For diversions, entertains,
Or to glean some needed gains.
When some lose they walk away,
Others even harder play

By increasing wagered stacks
Trying to win losses back.
For some, just a brief romance,
Courting this, a game of chance.

People-watching at its best,
As our money we divest,
Knowing odds are we will lose.
Canadian donation dues

To not-for-profits, charities
Helps disgruntled egos ease.
A 'dumb tax'? It may be so,
But chances are, next time we'll go.

THE DAY BEFORE TOMORROW

You'll get it all; you have my word.
I pay back what I borrow.
It will be soon; it's just deferred
From the day before tomorrow.

The pain would ease, she had been told;
Each day a bit less sorrow.
A brighter future she'd behold,
Except the day before tomorrow.

The bull had left him half-alive
Last year – Diablo Toro.
He wondered if he would survive
The day before tomorrow.

The youngster shoveled the manure
For the money to see Zorro.
And wished he hadn't to endure
The day before tomorrow.

The world can be a scary place,
With an uncertain morrow,
But first it brings us face-to-face
With the day before tomorrow.

BUGGED

Spring squalls, insects crawl
In your door and up the walls.
There through summer and late fall,
Till their own Grim Reaper calls.

Ants find vintage wine
And picnic fare on which you dine.
Their endless forage is the sign
To leave idyllic spot behind.

Cherries, raspberries,
Sweet and ripe, but in the trees
And bushes lurk the wasps and bees
Who'll sting unwary hands and knees.

Fruit flies patience tries;
Up your nose and in your eyes.
To open mouth now seems unwise,
Lest you ingest a winged surprise.

Cold blast here at last.
Shut windows, secure them fast.
Reminisce of summer past,
Forgetting how the bugs harassed.

Dwarf foes, mosquitoes;
Bugs are everywhere we go.
Through our lives they ebb and flow,
Footnotes in trials we undergo.

PART III: Social Scene

We often seem to lead boring lives, but to 'people watchers', we're infinitely fascinating. After all, where do we get more input (wanted or not) than from other people?

Below are observations made over the years, many of which provided insights into my own occasionally-mystifying responses to folks I have chanced to meet.

WOMANIZER

Save me; I'm believing all your wicked lies.
Save me; your appeal has got me mesmerized.
Redirect your devastating charm.
Tell me that's it's just a false alarm.

Spare me; I'm no match for your convincing line.
Spare me; catch a plane and leave me far behind.
This is not the time, is not the place.
Disappear from here without a trace.

Outlaw, don't you put your brand on me tonight.
Outlaw, I won't help you face the morning light.
Ride until you meet the rising sun.
I won't be a new notch on your gun.

A womanizing superman
Love interest now on almost every block.
No purpose, nor is there a master plan.
A wolf having a field day with the flock.

INSINCERITY

I ran into an aging friend
I hadn't seen in years.
We reminisced of times gone by
And swigged a couple beers.
Swapped lies re how well we had done,
And who we'd grown to be.
A dozen words to hide decades
Of mediocracy.

We parted then, each went his way
With vows to keep in touch.
Worse than strangers now, for we
Both had learned too much,
Seen failure and defeat within
One another's eyes.
The mask had slipped and stripped us of
Our verbal, glib disguise.

If only we had opened up,
Admitted our despair,
Faced each other and ourselves
And taken it from there.
But twin false egos reared their heads
In silence and self-pity.
Such is the heavy price we pay
For insincerity.

I'VE GOT A HOLIDAY

I've got a holiday all to myself
To while away any way I choose.
Sun on a stretch of sand would keep me well amused;
Who could refuse it.
One day so perfect that money can't buy
A single hour of this precious time.
To squander or spend,
No wonder I'm in
Fifth heaven and quickly ascending.

I've got a special friend who I adore
Who wants to help share my holiday.
He knows I wouldn't have it any other way;
What can I say?
There was another day just like today
When he consented to be mine
Through thick and through thin,
No wonder I'm in
Fifth heaven and quickly ascending.

ONLINE DATING

With fingers poised and hopes engaged,
We're back into the dating stage
We left behind decades before,
And wonder what Life has in store.

For those of us with faithful heart,
And boundless love for counterpart,
We trust the wait won't be in vain,
And we'll passionately love again.

A profile written to unveil
Just who we are: my name is Gail.
The many things I like to do?
Take photos, fish, and garden, too.

What else, you ask? I volunteer,
Write poems, novels to endear,
Like gentle hikes, and sand and sea,
With someone special; that's the key.

At 65, I'm told I'm cute,
Empathic, kindly and astute.
I'm healthy, strong at 4 foot 8,
And in life always pull my weight.

Now, fella, may I ask of you,
What do you want in someone new?
The next to be your current date,
Or single partner and lifemate?

I've never had much wanderlust.
Is warmer winters now a must?
Contemporary age, nearby –
Do those particulars apply?

If what you've read has turned your crank,
Don't let the Message box stay blank.
If I'm the one you've wanted so,
And you don't write, we'll never know.

GIVE IT UP

You've been drinking all day and swinging all night
With every Sally, Mary and Jane.
Money flowing like water 'neath the bridges a-burning,
Fire-water coursing through your veins.
Acting like a man with a week to live
Who knows his body ain't worth a dime.
Blowing your today like there's no tomorrow
Madly trying to recover lost time.

Sporting jeans too tight, courting janes too loose,
Trying hard to become what you're not.
Wearing glasses so dark you can't see where you're going,
To be cool you think you've got to be hot.
Walking with a wiggle that makes the girls giggle,
But they're really only laughing at you.
You're an old fool, daddy, from your pose to your clothes,
And that goes for your golden wig, too.

You get a sixpack of beer and a sexpack of girls,
And suddenly you think you're Don Juan.
Once the fog slowly lifts from the fields and your brain,
Both the women and your money are gone.
Odd how the 'good life' can feel so damned bad,
But there's always gonna be tonight.
Ignore the sorry tale your mirror and your body's telling,
Yelling with all of their might:

Give it up, old fool, give it up!

SUPERSTAR

He grew up in the house next door,
And we were in the same class at school.
He was average – no less and no more,
Not a genius, but nobody's fool.

Seeing him as I did every day
From back when we were both mere tots,
He was just a friend with whom to play,
Share secrets, fight about who-knows-what.

Friendship uncluttered by catch-words;
Not 'sweethearts', not 'girl-meets-boy'.
The only kids around, we were
More like each other's favorite toy.

As we grew up, like precocious elves,
Sand castles were washed away by the tide
Of discoveries about our worlds and ourselves,
Till we were worlds apart inside.

To reach our goals, we had to shed
What we were to become what we are:
I, a nurse and mother, happily wed,
And he a hockey superstar.

You ask am I thrilled to have known him,
To have shared, for a time, all his joy.
He was my friend, but he was his own 'him';
Not my boyfriend; just a friendly boy.

The idol of millions
Was once a kid, too.
He's a memory to me,
And a hero to you.

THE FIGHT

Poor self-centered people,
Stubborn to the end,
Knowing that they're wrong
But much too proud to bend.
Marching out the door
With their noses out of whack,
Realizing as they go it
Will be harder to come back.

Alone, they think the words
They now wish they had said.
Instead, with verbal swords,
They slew each other dead.
And now their wounded vanity
Is keeping them apart,
Their foolish pride concealing
Two lonely, broken hearts.

But still they play their game of wounded pride.
Like soap operas, it's the same old story:
They lock their anguish steadfastly inside
Because they lack the guts to say 'I'm sorry'.
How many fools throw happiness away
And shun their golden opportunity?
The game of love is not a game at all,
And none hurt others with impunity.

THE WHIMSICAL CRIME OF RHYTHM AND RHYME

He just wasted the day; a mere poet, I say,
When he could have been working a job.
A whimsical crime, I call rhythm and rhyme,
As he stays at home, dressed like a slob.

He's sure no go-getter; you could do so much better
Than link up to someone like him.
Choose a lawyer or vet, not some loser you met
And decided to date on a whim.

But Dad, don't you see, he's the right one for me.
His love letters poetically speak
From his heart straight to mine, and he's gentle and kind
With exactly the nature I seek.

I've gone out with the rich, but they don't scratch the itch
For a man with deep feelings and thought.
When for sweetness I delved, they loved only themselves,
And assumed that I, too, could be bought.

Keep your weathy pendantics, I found someone romantic
Whose gold can be found in his heart.
Blessed with talent galore, he'll be never a bore,
I'm in love with a man of the arts.

ELOQUENT SILENCE

"Do you like it?", wife asked, but then he
Hesitated that moment too long.
Now no matter what he might reply,
It is destined to be taken wrong.

Sister mentioned completing a book
And an eloquent silence ensued
From a skeptical sibling, but one
Who still wished to avoid being rude.

Best friends hadn't spoken in days.
Silent treatment that wounded them both.
Doing damage far worse than the words
One had written in pique in a note.

Spouses kept all their thoughts to themselves
To avoid disagreements and stress,
Growing further apart deep inside
Till their love could no more incandesce.

Choose your words with impeccable care,
Making sure that they come from the heart.
In the social interaction of man,
Communication's the most pivotal art.

SEE ME

When the moon runs out of magic
And the stardust leaves your eyes,
When my name sounds unromantic
And you start to realize
That I was never heaven-sent,
No angel wings have I,
You'll see my love the way it's meant,
From the heart, not from the sky.

Till the Earth's no longer quaking
When you see your perfect girl,
Till my smile's no longer making
Your head begin to whirl,
Till the mist that's fogging up your brain
Has cleared away enough,
You'll be up on Cloud Number Nine,
High on sex-appeal, not love.

See true-me, not just my beauty.
Seek my heart, rather than skin.
Let it be a pleasant duty
To find she who dwells within.
For I'm not just an outer shell;
You must look deep to see depth.
Love me, but like me as well.
When shape's lost, substance is kept.

THE CORNER ROOM

The Corner Office – how they fought
To ensure it's the one they got,
With windows all the way across,
The one earmarked for second boss.

We watched the squabbles and intrigue,
With who-all they were now in league,
The soldier-gathering at its worst,
The power hunger to come first.

And when the dust had settled down,
The most unworthy wore the crown.
We exchanged glances, for we knew
We'd do the work, he'd 'overview'

And reap the kudos for our toil.
To victors always go the spoils.
On our skills, he would move ahead,
Until the last of us had fled,

And a new crop take our place,
With dreams of carving out a space
Where they could demonstrate their worth
And move up to a higher berth,

Have others at their beck and call,
Who stoop to work while they stand tall,
And hope one day they would assume
Their rightful place in Corner Room.

HEART HUNTER

He saunters into the singles bar
With a half-smile on his lips,
Stands drinking in the *she*-nery
Like a connoisseur, in luscious sips.

His smile just oozes sincerity
(The better not to read his mind),
As he chooses his quarry – namely, you.
Watch out for his verbal traplines.

And you know it's just all an illusion,
And you know that he isn't for real.
No towel or ashtray memento for him;
It's your heart he's preparing to steal.

One part charisma, two parts champagne,
Innuendos, suggestions and lies,
Flattery to entangle your brain
While he's promising love with his eyes.

Oh, don't you become his Girl Friday,
'Cause Saturday's coming up fast.
He hunts for hearts instead of heads,
And leaves them, broken, in the grass.

APPARITION

She yipped, he gasped, they stared, aghast,
An apparition there
Before their eyes, form undisguised,
Quite terrified the pair.

No more alone within their home,
They worried and they fret,
What drew it here and kept it near,
And did it pose a threat?

Though daily heard, it spoke no word,
Now form was never shown.
'Twould softly sing or move something
To make its presence known.

In time they got to fear it not,
And call the phantom 'her',
Politely greet, and knocks repeat,
Acknowledge, as it were.

Then came the night, them sleeping tight,
She firmly shook their bed.
They quickly woke and smelled the smoke,
And from the house they fled.

They sold the land, moved nearby, and
Asked her to come along
To quiet street with added suite
All hers, for she belonged

Near them, they felt, for how she'd dealt
With saving them that night.
They gave her space, just cleaned her place
And furnished it up right.

They'd quickly known she wasn't alone;
Overheard excited chat.
She'd now a beau – a nice fellow;
A karmic tit for tat.

THE FOX

She walked into his lair
Unsuspecting, unaware.
Her first encounter
With such a bounder.
The answer to a dirty old man's prayer.
Enter the fox . . .

A pair of hooded eyes
Peeping 'neath his hair like spies.
Hunter and quarry
Urban safari,
The lecher is about to claim his prize.
Stalks, the fox . . .

He sees his chance and leaps
But she's faster on her feet,
And in the foray
She decks her quarry,
And steals his wallet, watch and two gold teeth.
Exit the fox.

ALONENESS (Aimed at Dating Sites)

For six long years, he has been gone.
I sleep alone from dusk till dawn,
And volunteer, to keep at bay
The loneliness another day.

I've learned a lot, created more
Than e'er I've done the years before.
Time packed with my activities,
I'm free to do whate'er I please.

No catering to someone's taste;
No compromises, mess or waste.
With well-filled days but empty nest,
The yearn to love goes unexpressed.

Elders often remain alone,
Rather than face the Great Unknown.
Too set in ways a lifetime built,
They let their loving nature wilt.

Or claim they're younger than their age
And think they deserve, at this stage,
Playmates who exude youthful zest
To help them perform at their best.

Others who note the march of time
Now seek a mate still in her prime
So when at his unhealthy worst,
He'll have for free a private nurse.

Is it so long ago that we
Can't recall what true ardency
Feels like, nor wish to recreate
The bond between two loving mates?

Well, I believe that senior men
Are capable of love again.
When 'eros' wanes, there's still 'agape'
Until we make our Great Escape.

Ye men who dream of something more,
Someone with whom life to explore,
A gal your age is bound to be
Seeking a fellow just like thee.

So all love hunters, gather near
And find yourself somebody dear.
Us lonely singles do abound.
What once was lost can still be found.

Pick up your courage, ask for dates,
From women with delightful traits.
If she makes you a happy man,
Then give her all the love you can.

TO SCORE A DATE

Invited to a party
Somewhere he'd never been,
He found the people hearty,
And cute girls unforeseen.

Unused to making contact,
He listened and he watched
To learn how women interact
With men who scored or botched.

One gal of special charm,
Approached by macho sleaze,
Accepted card. He tweaked her arm
As brazen as you please.

He left. She slipped the card
Beneath a nearby plate.
The shy young man tried hard
Not to grin at the jerk's fate.

Her perfect combination
Of beauty, sauce and spice
Ignited conflagration
Of ardor to entice

The young man to approach her,
Present his gentle pitch,
And hope he's not a poacher
In another fellow's niche.

A moment's hesitation,
His courage to deploy,
For minimal flirtation
Has he done, this country boy.

She turned to gaze upon him
As he hesitantly smiled.
He prayed to not fall victim
To her soft dismissal style.

"I have no card to offer you.
I didn't come prepared
To meet someone I'm drawn to,"
The man candidly declared.

She said, "Premeditation
Is an aggravating sign.
You've no card for donation,
So for now, I'll give you mine."

AND THEN THERE WAS ONE

So many, too many, unable to choose,
One goal or another, the vocation to use.
Join the family business or follow my friends,
My teachers or guidance instructors or trends.

The notions have plusses, though some very few,
When folks tell me what they believe I should do.
The others might feel like I'm letting them down
But I can't be it all, from CEO to a clown.

What would I dislike (let's approach it that way).
What'd make me reluctant to start each new day;
Where the thought of that future just wrinkles my nose,
And instead of rewards, all I see are the woes?

Become an accountant like my uncle and Dad
Would be far down the list for this new high school grad.
And I can't see myself through the counsellor's eyes,
With a landscaping business or fast-food franchise.

My mother's been hoping I choose doctor or law
Paid by scholarships, grants – whole financial hoopla.
Eight more years of schooling, 'no, thank you' to that.
And I'll be no one's flunky or a juvenile frat.

Friends have no ambitions, any old job will do,
So their evenings are free for a laugh and a brew.
But what does that leave, I now wonder aloud,
That will let me be happy and make myself proud?

For there was someone missing in advisers, you see;
That unplumbed resource was none other than me.
When I look at careers that merge profit and fun,
From the jumble I find there remains only one.

PART IV: All About Kids

Here are some humorous story-poems about the younger set. I am especially amazed by how accurately they can perceive things we long ago stopped critiquing.

THE JOYS OF PARENTHOOD

I never did like you. Ya wanna know what you are?

You're an accursed, aggravating, abhorrent, appalling ass.
You're a cruel, calculating creep, a cretin and you're crass.
You're depraved, disgusting, detestable, deceitful and dumb,
A foul, fiendish fink, a floosie, and you're fulsome.
You're a horrid, hideous, hateful, heinous whore,
Insufferable, intolerable, insidious, indecent, and more.
You're loathsome, licentious, lewd, and a lying lout,
Malevolent, malicious and mean, and you've a big mouth.
Obnoxious, odious, obese, offensive at best,
A putrid, perverted, pug-nosed punk, a plague and a pest.
You're a rotten, wretched, repulsive, revolting ruffian,
A stinking, shocking, sickening, sniveling scab, and
A villainous, venomous, vexatious, vile vixen!

What do you say to that?

You're a rat!

Mommy *(sob!)*, he called me a *rat!*

JASON

Jason was a little kid
Who simply did the things he did,
But wasn't sure exactly why
Things always seemed to go awry.
His parents scolded him a lot
And said the time-outs that he got
Would let him think out what he'd done,
Although he'd just been having fun.

So he decided, one fine day,
To pack his toys and move away.
He knew a house abandoned long,
So living there would not be wrong.
He took some sandwiches and meats,
Juice and cheese and tasty treats,
Some extra batteries for his games,
And all his tracks and model trains.

Of course, his teddy had to come,
But he would have to leave his drum
And nifty pool his Dad had bought.
He'd surely need his old slingshot
To protect him from the bears.
He packed slippers, underwear,
Jammies and a change of clothes –
Then the suitcase wouldn't close.

So he grabbed another tote
From the closet for his coat,
And remembered many things
He would also have to bring.
Soon that, too, was overfull,
And much too heavy, now, to pull.
He would have to run away
Slower then, a bit each day.

When finally it was time to go,
He realized his favorite show
Was starting, so he had to wait
And watch it, and then lunch he ate.
He should leave a note to say
Why he chose to run away,
But he couldn't then come back
To pick up his other sack.

Or a wheelbarrow to haul
Everything before nightfall
To the shack, deep in the woods
Where he'd hide his worldly goods.
He was getting in a flap
When Mom insisted on a nap.
Then she sent him out to play,
So he couldn't leave that day.

After dinner he unpacked
Toys and food and all the snacks,
And stored them in the old woodshed
Before he had to go to bed.
He'd pack it all again next day.
There *had* to be a better way.
Perhaps he'd just forget his irk,
'Cause leaving home was too much work.

OUR GAL SAL

At dawn she wakes, yawns and shakes
Her crown of shining curls.
" 'Morning, giggly, wiggly, wriggly, pretty
Itty-bitty merl!"
A sweet and simple, neat and dimpled,
Cute impudent gal.
Slick with tricks, a pixie of six
Is our sandaled handful, Sal.

A loving, laughing, living liebchen,
Frisky as a foal.
Azure eyes like mirrored skies,
And hair of ferrous gold.
She implores and plots and plans and schemes,
The better to get her way.
She whiles away the hours while
We toil away the day.

Blooming like an orchid, though she's
Growing like a weed.
Rambling, gambolling, rollicking, frolicking,
Busy indeed.
Rippling laughter, tripping after
A dragonfly hatchling.
"It's TinkerBell! I can tell
By the rainbows on her wings."

Night dark as soot, night owls hoot,
Time to scoot to bed.
Snuggle in with smuggled tin
Of cookies 'neath bedspread.
Long before she dares explore
The treasure in her hand,
Sky's velvet amber burns to umber,
And she's in slumberland.

HOBNOBBIN' WITH A GOBLIN

A kid was born on Christmas morn,
And Robin was his name,
A happy boy whose favorite toy
Would join him in his game.
Nobody knew exactly who
Had given it to him.
It just was there, 'most anywhere
He was, through thick and thin.

He'd wander out to walk about
With that one figurine,
Later that day, he couldn't say
Exactly where he'd been.
And that was why his Mum would try
To follow him around.
He didn't mind, 'cause what she'd find
Was certain to astound.

He heard her gasp, the hand he clasped
Had belonged to a doll,
And knew she'd see the toy that he
Was playing with grow tall.
It moved about and then reached out
To point to where she stood.
And Robin saw her growing awe
Now boded nothing good.

Quite horrified by what she spied,
His mother made a squeak.
She held her breath, turned pale as death,
Before she tried to speak.
"Come here quick, he'll make you sick.
You mustn't be hobnobbin'
With creatures foul that nightly prowl,
Like shape-mutating goblins."

Though he explained, her terror reigned;
She wouldn't listen now.
He had to leave his friend, bereaved,
But he'd be back somehow.
The goblin wept and sadly crept
Into a hollow tree.
Broke Robin's heart for them to part
So very tragically.

His mother bought new gifts but not
A one could take the place
Of Goblin Grim's mischievous grin;
Mere toys were just a waste.
So late at night, by stars alight,
They shared a window sill,
Two lonely friends whose chat depends
On hiding their free will.

"Come live with me inside my tree,
Like I have lived with you."
"I can't escape and change my shape,"
Said Robin, and he knew
The only way to spend their days
Together was to hide
Grim in his pocket, a toy rocket,
And to his Gramps confide.

The elder man would understand
And help them find a way
To convince Mum to let Grim come,
And in their house to stay.
They drove for miles, and all the while,
He worried about Grim.
What if Granddad would just get mad
And say, "Get rid of him!"?

In quite a sweat, Robin now regret
His ill-considered plan.
As they drew near, his growing fear
Bleached out his summer tan.
He swallowed hard, tried to discard
Imaged calamity.
When they arrived in Grandpa's drive,
He was nervous as could be.

With happy cries and dripping eyes,
His Mum hugged Grandpa flat.
Now Robin's turn, he saw concern,
And e'er the diplomat,
Granddad whispered so just he heard,
"We'll soon go for a walk."
Gave him a wink and juice to drink.
"And have a nice long talk."

For hours on end, it seemed, Mum spent,
Reciting ancient news.
Till Robin asked, at long last,
If he could be excused.
The garden called, and there he sprawled.
He let the goblin out,
Behind a willow so that fellow
Could in seclusion sprout.

"Who have we here?", his Grandpa's cheer-
ful query paralyzed
Both of them. No stratagem;
Their meeting compromised.
But before they knew what to say,
Granddad stuck out his hand
Which Grim now took, and then they shook,
A goblin to a man.

"You fear me not?" The goblin thought
This odd, for ne'er before
Had anyone this gesture done,
Or sought to find rapport.
"You're Robin's chum. Unlike his Mum,
I give each one his due.
If you're a friend to Robin, then
I'll be a friend to you."

"But how will we get Mum to see
Grim's doing me no harm?",
Asked Robin to their ally new.
"Get rid of her alarm?"
His Grandpa grinned and blew the tin
Whistle 'round his neck.
A she-goblin 'twas
(To Grim's applause).
"We'll introduce Miss Beck."

LUNCH

A slamming door and running feet,
Coat flying through the air,
Landing near, not on, the seat
Of the closest empty chair.

Bread and jars and buttered fingers,
Meat and spills and jam,
Pickles, cheese and off-key singers,
A broken glass, and "Damn!"

A mass of fingers, food and fuss,
Music, mutters, mess,
Reveals saporific lust
On a culinary quest.

And somehow, out of the debris,
A shape starts to emerge:
A sandwich towers precariously,
Trembling on the verge

Of counter's edge. It starts to topple,
But just before it lands,
It's snatched up by a couple
Of deft, determined hands.

Feeding frenzy time is nigh:
Flashing teeth, and *crunch!*
An orgasmically euphoric sigh,
And James has had his lunch.

THE EARLY YEARS

The trauma of change, as the new child is born.
Soon with clothing and blankets his body's adorned.
With parental pride, he is shown all around,
And attention is paid to each whimper and frown.

Before very long, the excitement has waned,
And he finds his behaviour being carefully trained.
What once was deemed cute is discouraged, and he
Discovers his place in his birth family.

By the time language comes, he's restricted by rules,
But at least better food has replaced tasteless gruels.
He can now eat in places he couldn't before,
Though he must not be crying or cause an uproar.

The next many years combine learning and play,
And he finds subtle methods to get his own way.
But it still isn't long till frustration sets in,
For in life's tug-of-war, it's now harder to win.

When approaching the time that he thinks he'll go mad,
He reaches 16 and gets a car from his Dad,
And his entire world changes – he has so much to prove,
Far less observation, plus the freedom to move.

So many temptations to avoid or partake;
So many decisions for his life he must make,
And clouding it all is a hormonal storm,
Rampantly triggered by cute feminine form.

With school almost done, there's his future to plan,
And he shudders to think that he'll soon be a man.
Without parents dictating how life will unfold,
It scares him to think what the future may hold.

For years he had yearned to be out on his own,
To succeed or to fail, his decision alone.
Now his parents' warning he recalls with dismay:
Take care what you wish for; you might get it one day.

THE ATTIC

Spooks and goblins lurk about,
As we search for hidden treasure.
The semi-light and semi-dark
Add atmosphere to adventure.

Old coins (in reality dubloons),
Swords, scimitars and old muskets
Convince us beyond any doubt
This was the home of a pirate.

An ancient chest with broken lock
Holds a rainbow of silks and lace.
Perhaps her spirit lingers near,
Phantom lady of Inner Space.

A windchime, almost choked with dust . . .
How it must have sung in the wind
'Board ship; and for it to be here
Our pirate must have been captain.

And he'd have made a treasure map,
As all famous pirates did.
We'll search this place until we find
The map, no matter where it's hid.

"Children, dinner's on the table.
The treasure will just have to wait."
Trailing dust, but with shining eyes;
That's how happy childhoods are made.

TOAD A LA MODE

Fat and dumpy, mega-lumpy, getting grumpy now,
Toad a-hopping, start and stopping, leap and plopping – wow!
Child excited, quite delighted, unrequited joy.
Newfound pleasure beyond measure, treasure to the boy.

Zip to lock it in the pocket, pride skyrocketing.
Legs propelling Jay to dwelling, plans are all gelling.
Clothing hamper sure would pamper, it couldn't scamper out.
Many a fly on windows die, will supply toady mouth.

Sit the new pet on the dinette, off to get ice cream.
He gobbles some and licks his thumb, tells his chum his scheme,
Then needs the loo (a number two), without ado departs,
Hoping his friend will not descend and from the kitchen dart.

Jay hurries back to eat his snack, is taken aback by
The sight of toad now a la mode, followed by father's cry,
"No ice cream topper is a hopper; it looks the proper fool.
I'd say offhand, its place to stand is on a tan 'toad stool'."

Where e'er Jay went, the toad augmented time they spent alone.
Off-work they'd play, the decades they enjoyed, tho Jay had grown.
None seemed to mind how close aligned they were, nor find it odd.
Most had a dog, cat or hedgehog. A toad? Different, not flawed.

You never know, when out you go, what life will throw your way.
So keep your eyes peeled for the prize, it could arise today.
And that new chum could look like scum, be crummy as a toad,
But stand by you, be tried and true, like precious few have showed.

WHAT'S IN THE BOX?

In total thrall, with widened eyes,
The child beheld the Big Surprise –
The one that all the hints foretold
He'd get, on turning eight years old.

With fingers clasped in praying stance,
And feeling like he's in a trance,
He held his breath, and dared not speak . . .
But had he heard a tiny squeak?

He wet his lips, as Dad approached,
Most patiently, as he'd been coached.
"Oh, hurry, Dad!", he begged within,
Still mute despite internal din.

And now the moment was at hand.
The box was passed to boy from man.
With admonishment to use great care,
For what's inside he mustn't scare.

It couldn't be! His dearest wish
Had always been to have a fish,
Or better yet, a rat or bird.
Could that have been the sound he heard?

With trembling hands, he slipped the bow
That held the box closed, then so slow
It hurt, he opened up the flap,
And gazed in rapture through the gap.

A blur of fur and wagging tail,
As through the opening it sailed,
A puppy dog! The cutest seen,
And he, the happiest he'd been.

With Mom and Dad crowded around,
He bubbled forth ecstatic sound,
Through laughs and tears, he heard them say,
"We love you, guy. Happy birthday!"

PART V: Pensive Morsels

Regardless of age, we all have wisdom to impart. Several of these entries were reminders to myself. I just found putting 'food for thought' in poetic form a more enjoyable read.

FIGMENTS

"It can't be done," the expert said,
And so claimed all the books she read.
A waste of time to even try,
With loads of airtight reasons why
A figment it would e'er remain,
The whimsy of a featherbrain.

And though she listened to the pro,
The idea titillated so
That she never put the dream away,
And wondered if perhaps one day
The way might finally be at hand
To build the wonder that she planned.

The decades passed, and suddenly,
Along came the technology.
Her innovation now progressed
From fantasy to full process.
When time and means at last collide,
The dreams of yore can be applied.

From my aphorism:

All human achievement was once a figment of our imagination. 'Impossible' is a figment of our beliefs.

THE FAIR

Come stand here by the window
And look out on the square,
At the milling population
All preparing for the fair.

See the food and festive trimmings,
See the banners flying high,
Platforms need to be constructed,
Tentpoles reaching to the sky.

Watch the faces of the workers
As they toil and sweat and cuss,
All the fuss that must go on to
Attract adult folk like us.

So we watch, like skeptic critics,
Efforts made to woo our presence.
Bands and singers practice softly,
Honing style and pitch and cadence.

Like juries we will sit in judgment,
Weighing everything for flaws,
Thus risking our own enjoyment
Through sophisticated gloss.

Just look out upon that plaza
At the laughing children there.
They seek pleasure, not perfection,
So their world is one big fair.

THE LAST THING . . .

How oft we say, with vehemence,
One thing, but mean another,
Bemoaning when that fate we get,
Versus the one we druther.

"The last thing that I want to be
Is a burden to my kids."
Then comes illness or senility,
And that's exactly what she is.

It *was* the last thing, right enough,
Desire that she declared
With fervency, and Life complied,
Though semantically she erred.

"I've cared for others all my life;
It's time one cared for me."
Before too long, she got her wish
Through a cranial injury.

Emotional decisions can
Bring forth fulfillment, so
Be certain that the meaning fits
Your goal for your tomorrow.

CHOICE

The world is our oyster,
And it irks us like hell,
Though we ogle the pearl,
We can't open the shell.
And many's the reason,
As we prod and we pry,
That we accept defeat
Every time that we try.

"Mom said we're too weak, and
Dad said 'don't touch knives'."
For the six-year-old kid – yes,
But for the rest of our lives?
"And are we deserving?
What gives us the right?
What would our friends say?
Is this a fair fight?"

We can answer our questions
And discover our truth,
Or recite old excuses
Hauled around since our youth.
We can reshape our future
Or play pawn to our fates,
But the oyster's indifferent,
And the pearl still awaits.

CREATIVITY

A sudden urge to gladly splurge
Free time upon a theme.
The impetus inside of us,
Now coursing like a stream

Through fingertips or dance or lips,
Creative juices flow,
Give form to thought, our boring lot
Extraordinary grows.

And so it starts – expressive arts –
Which titillate the eye
Or ear or voice, our craft of choice
That raise our spirits high.

Though lost or 'found', obscure, renowned,
We're better for the gift.
We share our gold of heart and soul,
With those our arts uplift.

THE DREAM

A beautiful dream haunted him from the start
And eventually evolved to a goal,
Majestically sailing the winds of his heart
And the emerald seas of his soul.

But the 'hows' and the 'whens' became barnacle binds
'Till the dream was encrusted with doubts.
Distorted and drifting 'mong obstacle mines,
He was in and could see no way out.

Always a lady, now envisioned a hag,
Just a source of despair it became,
With frustration its cargo and failure its flag,
It devolved to a nightmarish game.

The saying goes, 'where there's a will, there's a way',
But he focused on ways, not on will.
"Let your dream light your night and your will rule your day,"
Taught his soul, "And it will be fulfilled."

So the soul of the dream and the heart of the man
Reunited and shook off the rust.
The dream shimmered visions of a promised land
And the captain swore success or bust.

Obstructions, objections fled out of his way
As he zestfully pursued his prize.
Aggressively jubilant, work became play,
For a goal's simply joy in disguise.

And the goal, once attained, though beloved it was,
A mere trophy to set on the shelf.
The treasure was making his dream his own cause,
And then living true to himself.

METHUSELAH CONCEPT OF FUTURE-MANKIND

Fear and worry, in a hurry,
Anger, greed, boredom, need,
Stress that festers, trials and testers,
Twisted values, crises deluge,
Body's aching, head is breaking,
Pressure's rising, realizing
You want to shout, "No more! Time out!".

A quiet-waters classroom
On a pleasant afternoon . . .
A gentle voice now soothes the cares away.
Your eyes are softly closed
And the mind in deep repose,
While critiquing what the speaker has to say:

"The problems that besiege you
Come from others that you knew,
Perspectives you forgot but function by.
If they bring you only grief,
They're a falsehood, a belief;
To live them is to try to live a lie.

The perspectives which are yours –
That voice your brain ignores –
Can help you separate the wheat from chaff.
Once objective re the facts,
A person thinks, not just reacts,
And the self-defeated cry becomes a laugh.

As you turn your life around,
Reassessing 'lost' and 'found',
Imagine living eons, for you could.
Nothing wears the body out
But our sadness, fears and doubt,
And belief in guilt and have-to's, can'ts and should.

Take a century or more
Just to grow, mature, explore,
And let the untruths taught to you dissolve.
Invest all the time that takes
And forgive your own mistakes,
For they're part of your beginning to evolve.

As you think and act and feel
Who-you-are becoming real
In your world, your ideals will grow and change.
Spend a decade, two or three
On a goal, then set it free
And go choose another with a further range.

If you haven't guessed it yet,
You decide how long, when death.
It is not a morbid conscious guessing game.
Be pragmatic, patient, by
Choosing goals not set too high.
To enjoy the getting-there is half the aim.

The Methuselah Concept:
Be objective, clear, adept.
Life's a given; it's the *living* that's a skill.
What you think is what you've got;
You are three-dimensional thought –
A genie whose own wishes you fulfill."

FRIENDSHIP

We confide our guilty secrets and silly little fears,
Goals and dreams and get-rich schemes,
Angers, sadness, tears.
We wonder how they stand us, and why they stick around.
They see so much in us that we
Ourselves have never found.

No need to guard our feelings against their ridicule.
The truths we lie we're not judged by;
We're the fooled, not the fool.
They lend us their perspectives to recognize our worth,
To free the past, be free at last,
And find our peace on Earth.

They're there when most we need them, and let us help them, too.
Teach and learn and share, in turn,
That wisdom may ensue.
They magnify the pleasures, give meaning to success,
Won't let us falter, veer or halt, or
Settle for second best.

With those who warm our hearts so,
Our lives uniquely blend.
Those best of all we simply call
Our true and trusted friends.

IN DAYS OF YORE

In days of yore (and days of mine),
The nectar Youth on which we dined
Promised dearest fantasies,
The world whatever joys we please.

But as the years rolled slowly by,
We learned not everything we try
Would gain us preferred dividends,
And broken dreams don't always mend.

As teen perfection slipped away,
Our friend, the mirror, did portray
What time was doing to our form,
And hinted at the coming storm.

"You know, I just don't feel my age,"
We say, and wonder how this stage
Snuck up on us without fanfare,
And on the friends whose lives we share.

One day, a thought occurs to us,
Amid the aches and pains and fuss:
Our body's truly getting old,
The fire that stoked us growing cold.

Though bodies come and bodies go,
There's more to us than e'er we know.
As timeless, ageless creatures, we
Embrace immortality.

And we who think and we who feel
Explore our lives with mental zeal.
When bodies fail, we shall remain,
To chart a course and start again.

WORK AND PLAY

The gulf separating the words 'work' and 'play'
Are the attitudes we have about each:
Continual toil so that maybe one day
Enjoyment will be within reach.

Paying our dues 'till we've suffered enough
To feel we have earned our reward.
Responsible, disciplined, bending – we're tough,
But we're also unspeakably bored.

And the concept of play becomes foreign to us,
Like a memory paled to a dream,
As we rassle with stress from what-is and what-was
And lose sight of our innermost theme.

One spectacular day we may look at our life –
What we are, what we do, what we've got,
Our friends and our family, our joys and our strife –
The whole picture that makes up 'our lot'.

And if we would start it all over again,
What we'd want to retain from before.
Surprising how much we've already attained
We're too fond of to boot out the door.

The 'why's we assembled our world as we did,
The attractions foresook and forgot,
Remain in our hearts, deeply buried amid
Frustrations, have-to's and whatnot.

Those things we would change, for they serve us no more,
Quickly culled from the herd of 'for keeps'.
Reawakening vigour, our direction's restored,
And the Pilot's no longer asleep.

If 'play' is defined, then, as simply a way
To produce satisfaction or joy,
Anyone, task or thing that gives pleasure is 'play',
And our world's just a versatile toy.

WHAT IF?

What if a portal opened wide
That had been closed before?
A way to fulfill dreams denied,
We thought, forever more.

For we had tried our level best
And never could succeed.
What if our will remained suppressed,
New prospects, didn't heed?

What if the love we sought in vain
Encountered us one day,
And in the meeting of the twain
We simply walked away?

Believing ardor passed us by,
Would never come again,
We looked at love through jaundiced eye
Perceiving 'now' for 'then'.

As wine takes tenure to mature,
Our goals are time-attuned
Because they didn't come before,
Means not they won't come soon.

Time brings us chances unforeseen,
If we're vigilant and wait,
Expand our talents in between,
The futures we create.

SHIP

His boring job done for the day,
The young man went down to the quay,
As always, to look out to sea
Where he'd most prefer to be.

He chewed his gum and fantasized
About the future that he prized,
And dreamed the dream he knew by heart
The one that would set him apart.

Adventures that he yearned to live,
No longer sitting here, passive.
"Some day," he quietly intoned.
" 'Cause I can feel it in my bones."

Mother and child strolled down the dock,
A detour on their daily walk.
The boy sat right beside the man
Who looked down from his ocean scan.

"What are you watching?" the child asked,
As in the sunset rays he basked.
The man said, with a wink and grin,
"I'm waiting till my ship comes in."

"You mean that big one way out there?"
"I haven't got one anywhere."
The boy frowned, "Seems a little dumb,
To wait for something that can't come.

I put my coins in a piggy bank
Till I've enough to buy a tank
Or truck or a new video game.
They all take money just the same."

With that, the youngster walked away,
Not knowing what he'd done that day.
A wake-up call from youthful lips
In time became a fleet of ships.

RETIREMENT

No longer mired, you're now retired.
You've ditched that nine-to-five.
The dream transpired that you desired,
So into freedom dive.

Hobbies and cruises, what amuses,
Fills each successive day.
Old office ruses now defuses
And you're living life your way.

But before long, the urge grows strong
To put your mind in gear.
You cast around, and soon have found
A place to volunteer.

You get involved and problem-solve,
And end up on their board
To help resolve, issue dissolve,
Be part of the accord.

And then your deeds do somehow lead
To a goal you'd love to explore.
The plan you seed grows like a weed,
And you're busier than ever before.

Exercising the mind helps you to find
What it means to be truly alive.
To retire's not a sign of the end of the line,
It's re-engaging your zest and your drive.

A LIFE WELL LIVED

An infant is born, he's a healthy young boy.
His lusty first cry triggers parental joy.
He little by little accepts Earth as his home
And forgets the nine months that he spent in the womb.

His future unfolds as it probably should,
And he learns how to take all the bad with the good.
From a child to a teen at the warp speed of life,
And soon he has got his own daughter and wife.

A spirited race from the job to the pool
To skating rink, ballet, recitals at school,
Grocery shopping and yardwork to do.
Demands are too many and hours too few.

He drives her to college, which is many a mile,
And before very long, walks his girl down the aisle.
One day in surprise in the mirror he stares
At the volume of silver he now has in his hair.

The years streak on by as only Time can,
And it's hard to believe he's become an old man.
But his life has been good, so he never complains,
Just makes the best use of whatever remains.

With his bod breaking down, he makes final plans
For his wife and his kid, the grandchildren and friends.
With a satisfied smile, he inhales his last breath,
And his loved ones all weep as he slips into death.

While they emotionally mourn the departure of him,
He perceives through awareness that's no longer dim,
And feels through a selfhood entirely his own,
Role-playing immortal temporarily home.

FAITH IN FATE

Three gents sought out a tavern on a chilly, dreary night;
Two for the beer and checkers, one for the company.
The older player, shoulders hunched, bemoaned his sorry plight,
As game on game he lost with painful regularity.

"I cannot win for losing, no matter how I try.
Ill wind it was that blew me to this God-foresaken town.
Whatever can go wrong, it does; on that you can rely.
If you're born to lose, like me, life kicks you when you're down.

You take my brother, Richard, now; he always gets the breaks.
You'd think he's got a guardian angel – he just can do no wrong.
Too good to last, that's what I say. One slip is all it takes,
And Lady Luck will turn on him. Besides, the good die young."

A game finally went to him, to the great surprise of all.
He made a big to-do of it; he smirked and rubbed it in.
"You thought you were so smart, eh? Well, pride goes before a fall.
You're luck's run out, time took its toll. It's now my turn to win."

All eyes, with renewed interest, watched the faded checkerboard.
"I think my ship at last came in. God willing, it's my game.
I'll never curse my luck again, not a single angry word,
And thank my lucky stars tonight into this pub I came."

But the fellow made a blunder, and once again he lost.
"The other shoe was bound to drop; 'twas too good to be true.
A victim of his nature's man; the losers pay the cost.
Live by the sword, you'll die by it. Don't fight – they'll still get you.

I've had enough of it tonight – in fact, enough for life.
I'll head home, if the weather holds. It's getting pretty late.
Ah, well," he sighed. "We know we'll never leave this world alive."
Then, of the barkeep, asked, "Hey, Joe! Do you believe in Fate?"

COMPLIANCE / DEFIANCE

Boy triplets were born, and identical all.
Folks couldn't tell which kid was Dave, Bill or Paul.
But as time hurried by and their personas grew,
There became no doubt as to which one was who.

Dave was the 'angel', best sheep in the flock.
At others' direction he never would balk.
Pet of his teachers, his parents' joy,
To follow their rules was to be a 'good boy'.

Through constant compliance he discovered, once grown,
He was ill-prepared to decide on his own.
A ship without rudder, he soon ran aground,
And to dictates of others was eternally bound.

Bill was the 'problem', contrary, a mule,
A battle of wills, a perpetual duel.
Doing the opposite of what he was told
To prove to the world that he was in control.

Defiant of Father – he won't be like *him!*
Dad's cautious, so Bill's always out on a limb.
Father is kind; Bill behaves like a cad.
But to never be like him, Bill must keep watching Dad.

Almost unnoticed in the midst of them all
Is quietly confident third brother, Paul.
While Dave seeks direction and Bill acts like a fool,
Paul lives his own standards and personal rules.

He makes his own choices and goes his own way.
Those who'd oppose him he turns gently away.
With like-minded friends sharing true-hearted quests,
He follows his dreams, finding peace and success.

GIVE AND TAKE

We're pressured to give, and to give till it hurts,
Suggesting that it's tantamount to our worth.
If that be the case, on dispensing our haul,
With nothing to give we're worth nothing at all.

Those people who have a compulsion to give
Will find the world is an unfillable sieve.
Acquaintances, causes and users galore
With pleas and demands will line up at their door.

Doing and giving out all that they've got,
To help everybody climb out of a spot.
Perceived as resources, the extractions start.
When the source is depleted, the takers depart.

Lest givers seem martyrs and the taker a leech,
Remember: To live their beliefs both need each.
Without someone to take, the giver can't give.
(Symbiotic relation of how each one lives.)

If the giver and taker both learn how to share,
No one is depleted, and both are aware
No contest exists, therefore no one will lose,
And the bond is of friendship, not user and used.

PURPOSE

The hungers and yearnings of a persistent goal
Which tugs at the mind are the needs of the soul;
Egged ever onward, subliminally willed,
We're propelled by a purpose that must be fulfilled.

Comes there a time when one's focus has gone
From the matter of Earth to what matters beyond,
Till the mountains-turned-molehills disappear from our view,
And we know who we are, what is false, what is true.

But in breaking our bond with material gods,
Without purpose on Earth, we are swiftly at odds
'Tween reality here and reality there;
Know too much to go back, but enough to go – where?

Put a child in a playground, he'll immediately play.
That the game is a game doesn't get in the way,
For the purpose is fun and for getting a feel
Of him being and doing and expressing his zeal.

Put a man in a world he can mold with his thought,
And he'll rue its compliance and will value it not.
But the lesson's not lessened if it's real or a dream.
To experience self-expression is the soul's 'being' theme.

THE AVERAGE GUY

Bob shrugged and he said, with an audible sigh,
"I'm nobody special, just your average guy.
I like all the things that most other men do.
If that's not what you want, then I'm not right for you."

She cheekily grinned, as she reached for his hand.
"Oh really? Let's look at the 'average man':
In every way that he can possibly be,
He'd have to be like the majority –

In looks and in stature, in style and in stride,
His speech and his income, how often he lied.
From hygienic habits, to fears and his wife,
Each element of the most commonplace life.

Every decision, each action he takes,
Would have to reflect what most other guys make.
The lifestyle he lives, and the job he works at,
Type of friends that he has and the kids he begat."

Bob was chuckling now, with his eyes all alit.
"It would be pretty hard to make everything fit."
"And to top it all off," she said. "He'd really be
The rarest guy in all of humanity."